President of the
Underground Railroad

President of the Underground Railroad

A Story about Levi Coffin

by Gwenyth Swain
illustrations by Ralph L. Ramstad

A Creative Minds Biography

Carolrhoda Books, Inc./Minneapolis

Special thanks to Dr. Thomas Hamm, Earlham College, for his careful reading of and comments on Levi's story, and to the staff of the Levi Coffin House in Fountain City (formerly Newport), Indiana, for their attic to cellar tour. — G. S.

Text copyright © 2001 by Gwenyth Swain
Illustrations copyright © 2001 by Ralph L. Ramstad

This book is available in two editions:
Library binding by Carolrhoda Books, Inc.,
    a division of Lerner Publishing Group
Soft cover by First Avenue Editions,
    an imprint of Lerner Publishing Group
241 First Avenue North
Minneapolis, MN 55401 U.S.A.

Website address: www.lernerbooks.com

Library of Congress Cataloging-in-Publication Data

Swain, Gwenyth.
    President of the Underground Railroad: a story about Levi Coffin / by Gwenyth Swain ; illustrated by Ralph L. Ramstad.
        p.   cm. — (A creative minds biography)
    Includes bibliographical references (p.   ) and index.
    Summary: A biography of a Quaker man from North Carolina whose fearless work on the Underground Railroad helped thousands of men and women escape the cruelty of slavery.
    HC ISBN 1-57505-551-1 (lib. bdg. : alk. paper)
    SC ISBN 1-57505-552-X (pbk. : alk. paper)
    1. Coffin, Levi, 1798-1877—Juvenile literature. 2. Abolitionists—United States—Biography—Juvenile literature. 3. Fugitive slaves—United States—Juvenile literature. 4. Underground railroad—Indiana—Juvenile literature. 5. Underground railroad—Ohio—Juvenile literature. 6. Antislavery movements—United States—Juvenile literature. [1. Coffin, Levi, 1798–1877. 2. Abolitionists. 3. Fugitive slaves. 4. Underground railroad. 5. Antislavery movements.] I. Ramstad, Ralph L., 1919– ill. II. Title. III. Series.
E450.C65 S93 2001
973.7'115'092—dc21   00-008579

Manufactured in the United States of America
1 2 3 4 5 6 – MA – 06 05 04 03 02 01

Table of Contents

Author's Note

In the 1830s, a frustrated slave hunter was said to have remarked that his slaves had disappeared into thin air somewhere near Newport, Indiana. The slave hunter, so the story goes, reckoned that his slaves must have taken a ride on some sort of railroad that ran underground. How else could he explain how quickly his runaways had disappeared—with the speed of a train—or how silently they had traveled—as if they were underground?

The slave hunter was wrong, but the name stuck. The "Underground Railroad" had no rails or train cars. It didn't travel under the ground. Instead, it was a network of people who worked together to hide and transport runaway slaves on their journey north to freedom.

Levi Coffin was part of the network, and that same frustrated slave hunter called him the "President of the Underground Railroad." The nickname was odd because Levi Coffin and the countless others who helped runaway slaves were successful *even though* they never had a president or a leader.

Every man, woman, and child—white or black—who worked on the Underground Railroad was an equal partner. Levi and the others understood what Southern slaveholders would never grasp: that no one worker was more important than the other. All were essential links in a chain. That chain led thousands of black people out of slavery in the South to freedom in the North.

1

Blood and Sparks

Thunk! Thunk! Levi Coffin threw small logs and kindling onto the bed of the wagon. He waited for his father to finish sawing another tree and listened to birds chirping in the brier bushes along the Salisbury Road. Levi watched the birds fly freely from branch to branch. Being the only boy in a farm family, Levi spent most of his days alongside his father, cutting down trees, planting crops, and mending fences. This day in the early 1800s was much like all the rest. Except that on this day, the usual quiet was disturbed by the sound of rattling chains and the muffled rustling of dozens of bare feet on the dirt road.

Seven-year-old Levi looked up to see a chained group of slaves being herded down the road by a slave dealer. This was the first time Levi had seen a coffle of slaves up close. While the coffle passed by, Levi's father greeted the slaves. "Well, boys," he asked, "why do they chain you?"

One slave with an especially sad face answered. The dealer, he explained, was worried that the slaves might run off before they could be sold to plantation owners farther south. Many had been taken from their families, leaving wives and children behind.

Levi had seen slaves many times before in and around New Garden, North Carolina, where he and his family lived. But those slaves weren't in chains, being taken away from their families. As he watched the long line of men pass, all Levi could think of was how he might feel if his own father were taken from him. If being a slave meant losing your father, Levi was happy not to be one. And he was glad that his family didn't own slaves.

Levi was born on October 28, 1798, to Levi and Prudence Coffin near the small town of New Garden. Levi's family was a perfectly normal Southern farm family, except that no one in his family had ever owned slaves. The Coffins were members of the Society of Friends, and Friends (or Quakers) did not believe in owning people. This made Levi's family different from some of their white neighbors, like the Caldwells, who owned several black people. But it didn't make the Coffins enemies of slaveholders.

Quakers hoped to convince others to end slavery by their own example. The Coffins, like most Quakers, didn't force their views on other people. After all, no one expected slavery to end in their lifetime, so it was best to get along with the neighbors. In turn, slave owners around New Garden tolerated members of the Society of Friends because they were known to be honest people who kept to their own business.

Levi hadn't given much thought to slavery until that day on the Salisbury Road. But the image of the chained men stayed in the back of his mind. He thought of it again a few years later when he and his father traveled to the Yadkin River to catch shad. They camped at the edge of the mountains, where the water fell fast over rocks and rapids. The campground was owned by a family named Crump. The Crumps sometimes let their slaves fish at night after their regular work was done.

One morning a slave sold his catch of the night to Mr. Coffin and offered to bring him more the next day. Levi's father was just saying he'd be glad to buy as much as the man could catch, when one of the Crumps angrily walked up to the campsite. It was fine, if and when a Crump allowed it, for a slave to sell his catch, but to make a deal for the next night's catch was taking too much for granted. A slave who assumed he could fish when he wanted was an uppity slave, as far as Mr. Crump was concerned.

While Levi and his father watched in horror, Crump grabbed a burning stick of wood from their campfire and began hitting the man with all his strength. Blows fell on the slave's head and arms, front and back. Sparks flew and mixed with blood. The man screamed in pain.

Mr. Coffin called out to stop Crump from doing more harm. Levi was too shocked and scared to do a thing. In his heart, he knew that what Mr. Crump was doing was wrong. The animals at the Coffin farm were treated better, much better. But knowing something was wrong and doing something about it were two different things. Levi wanted to call out or grab the log from Crump's hand. Instead he ran into the brier bushes along the river and felt his chest rise and fall while he cried.

After that trip, when Levi saw coffles on the Salisbury Road, he started to wonder about each and every one of the men, women, and children in the chained line. Levi had plenty of time to wonder. Many slaves traveled along the road in the early 1800s. Cotton growers on Southern plantations needed more and more laborers, so slaveholders in Virginia and Maryland were selling as many slaves as they could spare.

Watching the long lines pass his house, Levi was reminded of families left behind. When he saw chained men with scars on their backs from past beatings, he remembered the Crumps and the Yadkin River. He wondered if he would ever be old enough and brave enough to do something to end such cruelty.

2

Days and Nights

At fifteen, Levi was tall and lanky and strong. Although his five older sisters—and even his little sister, Priscilla—called him a boy, he did a man's work on the farm. Levi worked hard, but he also liked to have fun. He joked and teased his sister Sarah. He listened in on the talk and gossip of older men when his father sent him to the mill in Greensboro to have sacks of wheat ground into flour. And he visited the neighbors whenever invited, even if the invitation meant work.

Barn raisings and cornhuskings were more like parties than work. Everyone for miles around came to lend a hand. Levi went to cornhuskings at the Caldwell plantation as often as he could. The food was sure to be tasty, and Doctor Caldwell was sure to talk religion or politics. At one such party, Levi stayed behind in the barn at the end of the day while

14

the other white people went to the big house to have their supper.

Some of the slaves helping at the husking were part of a coffle. A slave dealer had stopped in New Garden on his way south, buying and selling slaves on the journey. The Caldwells welcomed the dealer to their party, and he brought the slaves along. Levi knew the dealer wouldn't approve, but he had to find out more about the men and women going south. Maybe, just maybe, he could help them. Where were they from? Levi asked. Had they left family behind? Were they being mistreated? Levi's voice came out in a whisper.

One of the slaves sitting on the straw of the barn floor, a man named Stephen, claimed he wasn't a slave at all. He was a free black man from Philadelphia, he said, and he'd been kidnapped while he was herding sheep in Maryland. Lying asleep one night in a small tavern, he'd been tied up, gagged, and taken to Virginia slave dealers. It didn't matter how many times Stephen told them that he was a free man. The dealers were too interested in money to listen. How were they to know he wasn't just a slave with a clever story? they asked.

Levi was shocked but not surprised to hear what Stephen had to say. He had heard of such cases before.

16

But Levi never imagined that he would meet a kidnapped freeman right in his neighbor's barn. That very night, before leaving the Caldwells' place, Levi took their slave Tom aside. He whispered Stephen's story to him and asked if Tom could bring Stephen to the Coffins' farm. Levi wasn't sure just what he could do to help the kidnapped man, but he figured his father might know where to begin.

When the knock came on their door the next night at midnight, the Coffins were ready and awake. By candlelight, Stephen told his story while Mr. Coffin wrote it down. Knowing all the details of Stephen's story would be crucial, Mr. Coffin explained, if he and others were to bring the case to court.

Before day broke, Levi walked with Stephen and Tom back through the piney woods to the Caldwell place. Levi couldn't be sure he'd be able to help Stephen regain his freedom, but the look of hope in the man's eyes made him glad to be trying.

It took longer than Levi ever dreamed. Six months later, after the Coffins and many other Quakers hired lawyers, wrote letters, and looked into the facts, Stephen was free again. Levi wanted to help others escape the cruelty of slavery. But there were often times when he didn't dare help, no matter how much he wanted to.

In Greensboro one day, Levi entered a blacksmith's shop on an errand for his father. There, he saw a slave being fitted with a metal collar and handcuffs, all attached to a long chain. He'd seen worse punishments for runaway slaves. Some were fitted with bells that rang whenever they moved. Others were chained to heavy balls. But never had Levi been so bothered by the sight. This time he recognized the slave as one he had met on the Greensboro road not long before. The two had even spoken to each other. Now he could only look on in silence as the master questioned his recaptured slave. Hadn't the master always treated his slave well?

"Yes, massa," the slave answered.

"Then what made you run away?"

"My wife and children were taken away from me . . . so when I saw them go away, I followed."

The man's answers didn't satisfy his owner. The metal collar, handcuffs, and chains weren't punishment enough, either. In anger, the master grabbed his slave's hand and put it on the blacksmith's hot anvil. Then he hit the slave's hand with a hammer, beating it to a bloody pulp. That hammer seemed to nail Levi in place. He couldn't think of a thing to do or say. He stood trembling while the master hooked the end of the slave's chain to a wagon and urged the horses into a trot. If the slave didn't want to be dragged to his death, he would have to run as fast as he could. And that was what he did, for as long as Levi could see, on down the dusty road.

Levi shook himself and tried to put his mind on his father's errands. He knew he should have tried to stop the slave owner, but the laws of North Carolina were against him. He could go to jail for helping a runaway slave. Most of Levi's neighbors and friends—even those who were members of the Society of Friends—wouldn't have approved. They didn't like to interfere.

Levi's cousin Vestal, however, listened to the story of the runaway with interest. Vestal asked Levi to meet him one night in the pine thicket between their farms. When Levi parted the branches, he found that his cousin was not alone. For some time, Vestal had been helping kidnapped free blacks and even some runaway slaves escape to the North, where slavery was against the law. This was dangerous work, but Vestal was willing to take risks to help people escape slavery. Was Levi willing, too?

Levi didn't take long to make up his mind. Soon he was entering the thicket just before dawn or in the evening. He told his folks he was going to feed the hogs. And certainly, when Levi saw a hog, he fed it.

20

But he was more likely to give food to slaves who hid in the dense growth of pine trees. While they ate cold cornbread and bacon, Levi whispered words of advice about the road ahead.

Helping slaves was dangerous—and exciting. But in 1816, when Levi turned seventeen, the excitement wasn't enough. That year, Sarah Coffin died. The sister who had joined in his games, let him tease her, and become his friend wasn't there to talk to anymore. Levi's older sisters were married and starting families of their own. Only Priscilla was still at home, but she didn't have much time for her brother. At fifteen, Priscilla was popular, self-confident, and well on her way to becoming a minister. On Sundays, she spoke in Friends Meeting, and those who listened said she spoke God's words.

Levi knew he should be happy about his younger sister's success, but it only made him less certain about what direction his own life should take. He farmed with his father, but he didn't much care for farming. He had few ideas about other careers. Finally, one winter when he could be spared from the farm, Levi asked if he could go to school in New Garden. The one-room schoolhouse—with its rows of wooden benches, its maps, books, and slates—felt like home. Levi was a good enough student to think that he might become a teacher, but he didn't have Priscilla's confidence in speaking before a crowd, or even before one or two people.

That began to change, however, when Ede, the Caldwells' slave, knocked on the Coffins' door late one night. She was shivering so much she could barely speak. Only when Mrs. Coffin led Ede to the fire and pried her arms apart could Levi see the baby she was holding. Ede had run away from the Caldwells' plantation with her child. The two had been hiding in the thicket for several days and were cold and hungry and tired. The baby was sick, or Ede wouldn't have risked coming to the Coffins' house. Once Ede saw that her baby was warm and fed, with a place to sleep by the fire, she told her story.

The Caldwells' son, Ede explained, wanted a house slave to help his wife. The Caldwells had agreed to give him Ede along with her youngest child, the baby she was rocking even then by the fire. But Ede had three other children she loved just as much. And she had a husband who lived on a farm nearby. The Caldwells' son lived one hundred miles away. If Ede became his slave, she might never see the older children or her husband again. Which was worse, dying in the woods of cold and hunger or leaving her husband and her children without a fight?

The Coffins had been friends with the Caldwells for years. But Doctor Caldwell didn't look kindly on people—friends or not—who helped runaways. The Coffins were breaking the law. Levi figured he and his family were in almost as much trouble as Ede. Someone would have to try to convince the Caldwells not to arrest the Coffins and not to send Ede away. Before he had time for second thoughts, Levi volunteered for the job.

When he entered the Caldwells' comfortable parlor and sat on a stiff-backed horsehair chair, Levi's knees shook. He answered Doctor Caldwell's questions about family and school absently, trying to decide when and how to bring up the subject of Ede. Finally, he burst out with a question: hadn't their slave Ede run away?

Why, yes, answered the doctor. Did Levi know where she might be?

Levi didn't just tell the Caldwells where their slave was, he told them all about her nights in the woods. He told them how she'd slept in the cold on a bed of leaves, hardly daring to light a fire for warmth. Levi told them of Ede's fear for her baby's life and her love for all of her family. He explained how the Coffins had taken her in, hoping that they were doing the right thing even while they broke the law.

Levi couldn't remember talking for so long before, but he wanted to say everything he could to help Ede and to keep his family from going to jail. To be on the safe side, Levi threw in all the Bible verses he could remember.

Levi's nonstop talking and Bible quoting overwhelmed his audience. Young Mr. Coffin would make a fair preacher, Doctor Caldwell joked. "Well," he continued, while Levi stopped to catch his breath, "this is no doubt your first sermon, and you would be disappointed and might give up preaching if you are not successful; you may tell Ede to come home, and I will not send her away."

Doctor and Mrs. Caldwell chose not to prosecute young Levi and his parents. But the Coffins wondered how much longer they and other Quakers would be welcome in North Carolina. Some of Levi's relatives had already decided they could no longer live in a place where slavery was legal. In 1822, Levi's brother-in-law Benjamin White asked if Levi would like to come along on a trip west. Levi agreed on the spot. He was eager to visit a place where slavery was against the law, the rough frontier state of Indiana.

3

Lost in the Wilderness

It took five weeks for Levi and the Whites to travel
from New Garden to Richmond, Indiana, where many
other North Carolina Quakers had already settled.
The Whites set about building a home, while Levi
found a teaching job for the winter.

Although Richmond, in east-central Indiana, was a
frontier town, it wasn't new enough or rough enough
for Levi. At twenty-four, he was ready for adven-
tures. So when winter turned to spring, he left his job
to explore the heavily wooded lands to the west.

The main road leading to Indianapolis and beyond was little more than a rough trail. Levi headed toward the Wabash River, stopping along the way at lonely cabins. Near Terre Haute, Levi met his cousin Allen Hiatt. From there, the two traveled to Illinois, across a prairie wilderness of swamp and tall grasses and small clumps of trees. The trip started out well enough, but on the second day, the trail Allen and Levi were following abruptly ended. On the third day, they were nearly out of food and hopelessly lost. From their lonely campsite at night, Levi and his cousin could hear wolves howling, and the wolves didn't sound very far away.

When Levi and Allen finally stumbled upon a cabin on their sixth day, they were overjoyed. With good directions, they made their way to a settlement of Quakers. Allen stayed on, but Levi had had enough of the West. Once he found a good traveling companion, Levi rode to Richmond. He didn't stay there long, however. By October of 1823, he was back at the Coffin family farm near New Garden.

Since school had already started, Levi missed his chance of finding a teaching job for the winter. He was twenty-five years old—more than old enough to be living on his own—and instead he was back where he had always been, helping his father on the farm.

Soon he was too sick to care. A bad cold turned to pleurisy. Levi was so weak he couldn't work all that winter.

Sitting in a rocker by the fire at his parent's farmhouse, Levi felt almost as lost as he had out on the prairie. Being sick made him feel like a burden, and he still didn't know what to make of his life. Levi enjoyed helping slaves find freedom, but that kind of work didn't pay money. In fact, it cost money—money for extra cornbread and bacon, for jackets, and for shoes. If Levi wanted to help others, he needed a good job.

Late that winter, Levi got his wish. The people of Deep River, a settlement not far from the Coffins' home, needed a teacher at their school. They wondered, Would Levi take the job? As soon as he was well enough, Levi was teaching and earning good money. If he saved his salary, he could even make plans to move into a home of his own. And if he did that, Levi wanted Catherine White to be with him.

Levi had known Catherine, or Katy, since they were both children. Katy had a funny, dry sense of humor. She made Levi laugh the way he remembered laughing with his sister Sarah. She was also a Quaker, and she believed that slavery was wrong. When Katy agreed to marry Levi in 1824, Levi felt he had found someone who would share all of his life—the days of hard work teaching and the nights of helping runaway slaves and kidnapped free blacks. Levi was twenty-six when he married; Katy had just turned twenty-one. They rented a house near his school and settled in, for a while.

Both Levi and Katy understood that their time in North Carolina would be short. By 1825, all of Levi's family had moved to Indiana. Katy's family planned to move soon. When Jesse Coffin was born that same year, his parents started making their own plans. A slave state was no place to raise a child, Levi and Katy agreed.

Frost was in the air when Levi and Katy and Jesse began their journey over the mountains in September of 1826. Four weeks later, they arrived in Newport, Indiana.

4

All Aboard!

The streets of Newport, Indiana, weren't much to look at. There weren't many streets at all, just Main Street and Main Cross Street and a few others. Two dozen rough cabins and even rougher wood-frame buildings made up the frontier town. Hand-painted signs pointed to the few businesses that had sprung up: a saddle shop, a shoemaker's shop, a blacksmith's shop, and one or two taverns.

The town had no dry goods store, so Levi decided to try his hand at the business. It was too late in the year to find a teaching job, and a shop wouldn't take up much space. Levi and Katy fit their stock of cloth and rope, cornmeal and flour, and other goods onto a few shelves in their cabin. Business was good enough that Levi's family had plenty to eat that first winter.

Levi even made enough profit to think about expanding his business. Soon he had hired an assistant and was making salt pork to sell.

Levi was also asking people around town about another line of work: what, he asked, were Friends doing to help runaway slaves? Surely many slaves came to Indiana to settle or to follow routes farther north. Was anyone in Newport lending a hand? The answers Levi got surprised him.

There were three main crossing points for slaves heading north: Cincinnati in Ohio and Madison and Jeffersonville in Indiana. Runaways who crossed the Ohio River at any one of those points might pass through Newport on their way to Canada, where slave hunters couldn't follow them. But only the free blacks living in and around Newport were helping runaway slaves. Levi couldn't understand his white neighbors. Most had come to Indiana to get away from slavery, yet they didn't want to have anything to do with slaves.

Levi tried to convince white people in Newport to help out, but his neighbors had all kinds of excuses. Some argued that you just never knew about slaves: what if the one you helped had been a robber or worse? Others were afraid of what might happen if they were caught breaking the law. Most seemed happy that *someone* was helping the slaves, as long as *they* didn't have to do it.

Levi answered that the Bible said to help those in need. It didn't ask what color the needy were or say that you should only help the needy if they'd never done wrong. He told his neighbors that sometimes bad laws had to be ignored. And anyway, whites would always be punished less severely than the free blacks of Newport. Yet, after all his arguing and discussing, Levi alone among his white neighbors was willing to open his doors to runaway slaves. Katy was willing too, so by the end of 1826, the Coffins were welcoming runaways to their home.

Levi's neighbors were hard to convince. But in towns and cities throughout the North, more and more people—both black and white—were aiding escaping slaves. At first the aid was informal. If someone who looked like a runaway was found hiding in a farmer's field, the farmer might feed the slave, offer shelter until nightfall, and then show the slave the way to the next town. Or a sympathetic person might direct a suspected runaway to "the redbrick house with the basement kitchen," where someone else could help.

Some of the people who helped runaway slaves were Quakers, like the Coffins. Many were not.

Often the first people to lend a hand to slaves on the run were free blacks.

Gradually, as families like the Coffins learned of other families in nearby towns, they set up a kind of network of safe houses leading to Canada. At any one of those houses, people like Levi and Katy waited for a gentle knock on the door at night that might mean a slave needed shelter. They offered food, warm clothes, a place to rest. They often readied their wagons, hiding slaves under bales of hay while they drove to the next safe house.

Soon this network had a name. In the 1830s, one frustrated slave hunter called it the "Underground Railroad," since it seemed as if the runaways traveled fast as lightning and disappeared underground. The name stuck. In Newport, Levi and Katy's house was the railroad's Grand Central Station, and as Levi put it later, "there was no lack of passengers."

Levi and Katy acted mainly as "stationmasters." They often relied on Newport's free blacks to be "conductors," driving runaways in Levi's wagon, or leading them to safety on horseback. If a large group of slaves was traveling at once, a stationmaster might send a message ahead. "A large shipment will be arriving by Sunday," a message might read. The messages gave some information but not enough to raise suspicions. That was just as well, since slave hunters nosed around the Coffin home and other stations on a regular basis.

Levi called the men who hunted runaways for a fee "bloodhounds in human shape." A slave hunter who suspected someone of helping a runaway was likely to hand out his own rough justice, given a chance. Levi knew this, and at times it made his blood run cold with fear. But as he sent more "passengers" along the railroad, Levi learned to master his fears. He was never, he knew, as scared as the slaves were. And as long as he was doing right, he figured God would see that no harm came to him.

Just to be on the safe side, Levi learned all about the laws concerning slavery. That way, he could use the law to keep slave hunters from his door. Before a slave hunter could search a house, he had to have a search warrant and proof that he owned (or was acting for the owner of) a slave he thought was inside. If he didn't have those papers, he had to get papers from the local judge. But proof was often hard to come by, and the local judge liked Levi better than he liked slave hunters from the South. Luckily for Levi and Katy, people in town also started warning them when slave hunters were asking questions, so the Coffins had time to move slaves quickly to the next station.

The Coffins were lucky, too, that their store did so well. Helping slaves was expensive. Every visitor was hungry, so the Coffins always had to have extra food on hand. When large parties of slaves arrived, Levi often rented a second wagon to take them to the next station. For her part, Katy cooked food and made sure the runaways were dressed warmly. She even convinced some of her neighbors to help slaves by joining a sewing circle at her house. Together the ladies sewed and remade trousers and shirts to replace the rags many runaways wore.

Katy kept busy, but it didn't keep her happy the way it did Levi. When their second son, Addison, died in 1830, both were saddened. When a third child, Thomas, died before his first birthday, Katy's sadness wouldn't go away. Jesse was nearly all grown up. He didn't need his mother so much anymore. Levi seemed to have more time for slaves than for his own family. Katy tried to fill her days with sewing and cooking and working at the store, but the hours stretched on. The only thing that seemed to distract her was chatting with Jacob Hockett, a Quaker who helped out at the Coffins' store.

No one knows when Katy and Jacob decided that they were in love, or how Levi first heard of their feelings for each other. But in November of 1835, Katy and Jacob were thrown out of the local Quaker meeting for having an affair.

After the first burst of anger and hurt passed, Levi tried to look at things calmly. He wasn't sure he could blame Katy. When, between his daytime business and his nighttime work, had he found time for her? He had to admit that lately he hadn't been much of a friend. And who was more important to him than Katy White, the girl he had known since childhood?

The two worked together to patch things up. After all, they still cared for each other and for Jesse, and they shared a firm belief that slavery was wrong. Katy and Levi threw themselves into their work on the Underground Railroad, but they also tried to find time to be more of a family. In less than a year, Katy gave birth to Henry, a healthy baby boy. Not long after, two girls—Anna and Sarah—followed.

While Katy balanced feeding babies and cooking for runaways, Levi looked at the ways in which slavery seemed to creep into everyday life. A quick glance around any home in Newport revealed many things, some sold in the Coffins' own store, produced by slave labor. Frontier cooks baked with slave-made sugar. Women sewed cloth woven from Southern cotton. Farmers used slave-made rope to tie up their cattle. The products of slavery were everywhere.

Levi figured that if people opposed slavery, then they might want to buy goods that were made by free workers—not slaves. So beginning in the 1840s, he started stocking only free-labor goods in his store. Levi found plenty of customers in the area, even though his prices were sometimes higher than those at other stores. One year, he advertised that his stock of cloth included "a much better assortment of cotton goods than could be obtained last year, at prices considerably reduced, leaving no excuse for purchasing slave labor goods."

He was so successful—and his family so large—that he was soon looking for a new home. The house at the corner of Mill Street and Main Cross Street seemed just right. The large, two-story home was built of bricks, not logs. Levi even managed to work some free labor into the house. A free black man did much of the plasterwork.

A well room inside the house, next to the basement kitchen, would let Levi and Katy draw the extra water needed for runaways, without drawing the attention of passersby. Upstairs, behind one of the bedsteads in the girls' room, was a small doorway. The doorway was no more than three feet high, but it led to a long, windowless, secret room under the eaves. From the street, no one would suspect that the room was there.

If slave hunters managed to get the necessary papers to search the Coffins' home, that room could safely hold at least a half-dozen people.

When the Coffins settled into the house on Main Cross Street, they fully expected to live there for the rest of their lives. But by 1846, Levi wasn't sure they would ever own a home again. Things had been going so well with his dry goods business that Levi had speculated on pork futures. He had bet that pork prices would rise to a certain point and that he would make some money on that bet. At first, Levi guessed right. After a while, he had guessed right so often, Levi didn't think luck had anything to do with it. He had been making money, year in and year out. But in 1846, when prices didn't rise at all, his luck ended.

Levi was broke and disappointed with himself. How had he let himself gamble away his family's future? Where would he and Katy and the children live? And how could he go on doing the work he loved the most—helping slaves—when he had no home and no money? Levi hoped he would find some answers soon.

5

A New Start

Levi traveled to Salem, Indiana, that fall not because he wanted to but because he thought he should. He was going to a convention for people who sold free-labor goods. On the first day of the convention, he voted along with the others to raise three thousand dollars, even though he was too broke to chip in. The money would go to anyone who would set up a warehouse in Cincinnati. Levi and other free-labor storekeepers had trouble getting enough rope and sugar and cloth for their customers—all because there was no place nearby to store larger quantities. With a warehouse and with someone working hard to keep it stocked, free-labor stores might do even better business than stores that stocked slave-made goods.

On the second day, the convention voted to ask Levi Coffin to do the job. Levi certainly could use the work, but he had never given any thought to running a warehouse. At forty-eight, was he too old to be starting from scratch?

Whatever doubts Levi had, the next spring he and Katy and the youngest of their children moved into a house and warehouse on the corner of Sixth and Elm Streets in Cincinnati. Almost as soon as Levi had unloaded the family's furniture and boxes from the wagon, he was busy stocking the new warehouse with free-labor goods. Levi's business card said that he was a "merchant and dealer in free-labor cotton goods and groceries." But he was much more than just a grocer. In his new line of work, Levi used all the planning and organizing skills he'd gained helping slaves find freedom.

Just to get the cotton for free-labor yarn and muslin, Levi had to travel halfway across the country. First he made several trips to the South, trying to find cotton farmers who were either too poor or too opposed to owning people to use slave labor. Then he convinced Quakers in Indiana and back east to give him money to buy a cotton gin. Levi took the gin south to Mississippi and hired a man to run it. Next, Levi arranged to buy raw cotton and have it put through the cotton gin, which separated the white cotton fibers from the cotton seeds.

Levi did all this work without any slaves involved. He shipped the cotton to Memphis, the closest river city where he could count on finding free workers to load a boat. From Memphis, he sent the cotton—on boats where no slaves worked—to a northern factory. Levi had gone to the factory earlier to arrange for the cotton to be spun into yarn and twine and candlewicks, turned into batting for quilts, or woven into fine muslin cloth.

The quality was excellent, just as good as that of slave-made cotton. But to Levi, the quality was even better, since a person could buy his cotton and feel no guilt about supporting slavery. In fact, Levi maintained that buying free-labor goods might just end slavery. After all, slaveholders only wanted to make a profit from the work of their slaves. The more free-labor goods people bought, Levi argued, the less of a market slaveholders had. And the less money slaveholders made, the less reason they had for owning slaves in the first place.

When Levi and Katy moved to Cincinnati, they doubted that runaway slaves would still need their help. In such a big city, wouldn't the Underground Railroad already have plenty of workers? But once Levi started asking around, he discovered that the need for stationmasters and conductors was great.

Runaways frequently crossed the Ohio River to Cincinnati from Covington, Kentucky, and other Southern towns nearby. They came by rowboat, steamboat, ferryboat, or canoe. Some swam across in the warmer months, while others risked crossing on the coldest winter nights, jumping from one block of river ice to another. When they arrived, hungry and tired, they often went first to the homes of free blacks on the edges of the city. From there, white conductors like Levi Coffin generally took them into their homes to hide for a few days. Once slave hunters slowed their searching, Underground Railroad workers could send the runaways to the next town to the north.

Hiding slaves in a big city like Cincinnati might seem easier than hiding them in a small town like Newport, but Levi and Katy soon learned otherwise. Back in Newport, friends and neighbors were quick to warn them of a slave hunter's approach. In Cincinnati, the neighbors were as likely to support slavery as oppose it. Back in Newport, Levi was known to all the judges and lawmen for miles around, and most of them liked Levi better than Southerners. Cincinnati was a city on the border between North and South. Levi couldn't count on local judges and sheriffs to sympathize. Just over the river in Kentucky, Levi would find even less sympathy.

There, as he put it, "a negro-stealer...was looked upon as worse than a horse-thief."

The Coffins moved to Cincinnati when laws about runaways were changing. As far as Levi was concerned, those changes were all for the worse. In 1850, the United States Congress passed the Fugitive Slave Law to slow the growing fire of rage among Southern senators and congressmen. Southerners were more and more angry at Northern abolitionists, people who wanted to end slavery. Under the Fugitive Slave Law, the penalties for helping runaway slaves were made stiffer than ever before.

To protect themselves and their passengers, Levi and other conductors looked for new ways to hide and transport runaways. If they had to send a group of slaves north and they knew that slave hunters were watching, they might send a decoy buggy first. Levi and other workers, posing as white slave owners, might also escort their "slaves" to private rooms on steamboats moored at Cincinnati's docks, lock them in for safekeeping, and then leave the boat before it headed north. Once, Levi and John Hatfield, a free black, hid a group of twenty-eight slaves in two funeral wagons that slowly rolled through the city.

Every time Levi heard that another "shipment" had outrun the slave hunters, he felt like celebrating. One more slave had made it around the nation's laws and found freedom. Success made Levi so happy, he wanted to share the feeling. Soon he was going from door to door asking friends, neighbors, and business owners to "take stock" in a railroad. This railroad, he explained, had no engines or cars. But it did have cargo, and Levi needed money to ship cargo north.

Levi was persuasive. For a few dollars a share, many people in Cincinnati bought "stock" in the Underground Railroad. Afterwards, Levi visited shareholders to report on various shipments.

Usually, Levi had good news to report. While they lived in Cincinnati, the Coffins helped more than one thousand runaways. Levi had so many successes that it almost seemed as if he couldn't fail. But sometimes things went horribly wrong.

On a cold January night in 1856, a group of slaves crossed the frozen Ohio River and found their way to the home of a free black man named Kite. Kite went to Levi's house for help and advice as soon as he dared. Move the slaves away at once, Levi warned. He had already heard that the sheriff was forming a posse to track down the runaways. Kite hesitated. It was too light out to transport all the slaves together safely. And the group didn't want to be split up. Along with an older couple was a man, Robert

Garner, his wife, Margaret, and their four children.

Levi and Katy waited at home for Kite to come back with the slaves, but their wait dragged on. Before long, someone told them the news: as soon as Kite had returned to his cabin, a posse surrounded the place. Pistols cracked and popped in the cold morning air. Inside the cabin, everyone was in a panic. Margaret Garner, perhaps sensing that nothing could save her and her children, grabbed Kite's long butcher knife. As the posse broke down the door, she slit her older daughter's throat. Margaret tried to kill the other children and herself, but she had no time. The sheriff's men overpowered her.

Like most Quakers, Levi didn't believe it was right to kill another person, no matter what the circumstances. He tried to forgive Margaret Garner for what she had done, but at first he found it hard not to think of her as a monster, as so many other people in Cincinnati did. She was not large, only five feet tall. As long as Levi knew her, she never smiled. Her forehead and cheek each bore a scar. Levi asked about them, but Margaret said only, "White man struck me."

When Margaret appeared in court, the judge ruled quickly and decisively. The case was a simple matter of property, he said. And this property needed to be returned to its owner at once.

49

Levi's feet dragged while he followed the wagon carrying Margaret and the other slaves to the Kentucky ferry. He stood on the wharf and watched as the boat grew smaller and smaller. The wind was cold, but it wasn't the cold that made Levi shiver. It was the look on Margaret's face. Margaret Garner's capture was Levi's greatest failure. All he could do was keep trying—both day and night—to end slavery. That way, no mother would ever again have to make such an awful choice.

6

Traveling On

In Cincinnati and in other cities and towns, slavery was often a topic of discussion. At church suppers, on school playgrounds, and at family dinners, people in the North debated what to do about the millions of people living in slavery in the South. Abolitionists like Levi insisted that slavery should be abolished right away. Slaves should be given rights as citizens, Levi argued, although he didn't think blacks should be free to do certain things, like marry whites. Others, including a Congressman from Illinois named Abraham Lincoln, thought it would be best to send slaves back to Africa. Still more Americans thought that the future of Southern slaves should be left to their owners.

By 1861, it seemed to Levi that the slavery question was tearing people apart. Shots were fired that spring in South Carolina, and soon the country was at war. Southerners would battle Northerners for the next four years in the Civil War. They fought over the right to own slaves and over the rights of states to run their own affairs, without answering to the U.S. Congress.

At first, the Union and Confederate armies fought mostly in the East. Levi's life and work hardly changed at all. Lodgers kept coming, and so did runaway slaves. But by the fall of 1862, the horrible reality of war had come close to home. Union and Confederate troups gathered in Kentucky and Tennesee. After bloody battles, slaves ran for safety behind Union lines. The slaves hoped for freedom, but at first Northerners weren't exactly sure how—or if—to help the runaways. The confusion of war made resettling slaves difficult. Some were loaded onto boats and simply dropped off at the Cincinnati wharf with no food or money or shelter. Many others crowded into refugee camps.

The war and the confusion it left behind swelled into a flood, while Levi's Underground Railroad work slowed to a trickle. In 1862, President Abraham

Lincoln announced that he would make a proclamation on the first of the year, 1863. The Emancipation Proclamation would free slaves living in states still at war with the Union. Lincoln hoped to encourage slaves to come north and join the Union army, and many did. But many others clogged the roads leading north or crowded into refugee camps, making a bad situation even worse.

Levi visited one of the best of the camps in Cairo, Illinois, in December of 1862. But the "best" camp was one of the worst places he'd ever seen. People jammed into poorly built huts with no way of keeping warm and only a few ragged quilts for bedding. Most had run to Union lines with only the clothes on their backs. They had no pots and pans for cooking, no warm winter clothes. Smallpox was killing young and old alike. When Levi left that camp, he realized he had a new job.

Back at his desk in Cincinnati, Levi wrote letters as fast as his pen could move across the paper. He asked Quakers in Indiana and Ohio to send him dry goods, blankets, clothes—anything they thought freedmen could use. And he called a meeting of people interested in helping. The Western Freedmen's Aid Commission was formed before the month of January had ended.

Once again, Levi was organizing and planning, moving goods from one place to another, and helping people as best he could. That first winter, Levi and the Freedmen's Commission concentrated on sending food and clothes. Katy helped mend shirts, sweaters, and trousers, filling crate after crate. With permission from General Ulysses S. Grant, commander of the Union army, Levi shipped the goods by train to freedmen's camps. Levi and others realized that the freedmen needed more than just a full stomach and a warm jacket. Soon he was sending volunteers with books and school supplies to teach reading and math.

Near the end of May 1863, Levi traveled as far south as Corinth, Mississippi, to visit freedmen's camps and to find out what more was needed. He met freedmen with few tools who were struggling to plant crops at a camp in Illinois. In Memphis, he met others who were trying to hold church services and reading classes in an arbor made of brush. At LaGrange, Tennessee, he met people who were sleeping in the open. Tents hadn't arrived for them yet, and they had only quilts to put between themselves and the cold, dewy air at night. Yet none of the former slaves complained. Their journey from slavery to freedom was going to be a long one, full of uncertainties. Levi hoped he could help.

As Levi went from camp to camp, sometimes his way was blocked. He could hear cannons booming in the distance and saw wounded soldiers lying on the decks of steamboats passing by on the river. When things got bad, he prayed that he might just get back safely to Cincinnati and Katy. He was nearly sixty-five years old, but Levi had never felt younger or more alive. The Underground Railroad was closed, but Levi Coffin was traveling on. It seemed to him as if his work had just begun.

Afterword

Levi Coffin continued to work on behalf of the slaves until 1865, when the Civil War ended and the Thirteenth Amendment to the United States Constitution was ratified. That amendment completed the work of Lincoln's Emancipation Proclamation and abolished slavery. While people celebrated the new amendment, Levi decided that "it was fitting to resign my office as President of the Underground Railroad."

Levi and most other stationmasters and conductors didn't say much about the Underground Railroad in the years just after the Civil War. Southerners weren't soon going to forgive those who had worked to end slavery. Many people who met Levi in the late 1860s and 1870s didn't suspect that he had helped over three thousand men, women, and children find freedom.

But when he was in his late seventies, Levi began to reflect on his life. So many years had passed. He wanted to tell the story of his work on the Underground Railroad before he forgot the details. Over many weeks, Levi told his story to a young relative who wrote it down on paper. It was published in 1876 as *Reminiscences of Levi Coffin.* Levi died not long after in 1877, leaving behind a wealth of stories about the people and places of the Underground Railroad.

Bibliography

Books

Coffin, Levi. *Reminiscences of Levi Coffin.* New York: Arno Press and *New York Times,* 1968. Reprint of Third Edition, 1898.

Coffin, Louis. *Coffin Family Genealogy.* Nantucket, MA: Nantucket Historical Society, 1962.

Elliott, Errol T. *Quakers on the American Frontier.* Richmond, IN: Friends United Press, 1969.

Filler, Louis. *The Crusade Against Slavery, 1831–1860.* New York: Harper & Brothers, 1960.

Hilty, Hiram H. *Toward Freedom for All: North Carolina Quakers and Slavery.* Richmond, IN: Friends United Press, 1984.

Taylor, Robert M., Jr., and Connie McBirney, editors. *Peopling Indiana: The Ethnic Experience.* Indianapolis: Indiana Historical Society Press, 1996.

Manuscripts

Special Collections. Lilly Library, Earlham College, Richmond, IN. Huff-Nixon Family Papers (1760–1976). Clippings file related to Levi Coffin.

Pamphlets

"Grand Central Station, Levi Coffin House, National Historic Landmark, Newport, Indiana, (Now Fountain City)." Undated.

Huff, Robert N. "The Levi Coffin House, National Historic Landmark, Fountain City, Indiana, (Formerly Newport), 1839–1847." Undated.

Correspondence

Hamm, Dr. Thomas D. Personal correspondence with author, Special Collections, Lilly Library, Earlham College, Richmond, IN.

Mundell, Eric. Personal correspondence with author, William Henry Smith Memorial Library, Indiana Historical Society, Indianapolis, IN.

Websites

Levi Coffin House
<http://www.waynet.org/nonprofit/coffin.htm>
This web page includes inside and outside views of Coffin's Newport, Indiana, (now Fountain City) home. Links lead to related websites.

National Underground Railroad Freedom Center
<http://www.undergroundrailroad.com>
Part of the Underground Railroad history center in Cincinnati, Ohio, this website offers news and information on the Underground Railroad.

Index

About the Author

When **Gwenyth Swain** began researching the life of Levi Coffin, she discovered that Levi's family and her family covered a lot of the same ground. Coffins and Swains were among the first European settlers on the island of Nantucket. And Coffins and Swains ended up settling in Quaker communities in central Indiana during the early and mid-1800s. Ms. Swain doesn't know for sure if any of her Quaker ancestors were involved in the Underground Railroad, but she has enjoyed this opportunity to learn more about how the railroad was run.

A writer of biographies and picture books for children, Ms. Swain lives with her family in St. Paul, Minnesota. She is also the author of *Civil Rights Pioneer: A Story about Mary Church Terrell* and *The Road to Seneca Falls: A Story about Elizabeth Cady Stanton.*

About the Illustrator

Ralph L. Ramstad has been drawing pictures "since the age of three." He enjoys combining research with creative work. "Histories and biographies, particularly of the eighteenth and nineteenth centuries, . . . are my great favorites." Mr. Ramstad studied at the Pratt Institute in Brooklyn, New York. For 42 years, he created art for product packaging, print advertisements, and billboards. He has also illustrated several biographies and histories for Carolrhoda Books, including *Science Fiction Pioneer: A Story about Jules Verne* and *With Open Hands: A Story about Biddy Mason.* Mr. Ramstad lives with his wife in Minneapolis, Minnesota.